Annie Oakley
Saves the Day

written and illustrated by
Anna DiVito

Aladdin

New York   London   Toronto   Sydney

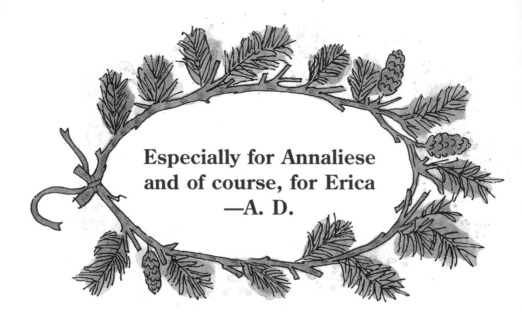

Especially for Annaliese
and of course, for Erica
—A. D.

First Aladdin edition November 2004
Text and illustrations copyright © 2004 by Anna DiVito

ALADDIN PAPERBACKS
An imprint of Simon & Schuster Children's Publishing Division
1230 Avenue of the Americas
New York, NY 10020

All rights reserved, including the right of reproduction in whole or in part in any form.

READY-TO-READ is a registered trademark of Simon & Schuster.

Book design by Lisa Vega
The text of this book was set in 18-Point Century Old Style.

Printed in the United States of America
11

DiVito, Anna.
Annie Oakley saves the day! / by Anna DiVito.
p. cm.—(Ready-to-read childhood of famous Americans)
Summary: While their father is away, young Annie Oakley and her brother
John help their mother during a blizzard.
ISBN 0-689-86521-X(lib. ed.) ISBN 0-689-86520-1(pbk.)
0121 LAK
1. Oakley, Annie, 1860-1926—Childhood and youth—Juvenile literature. 2. Shooters
of firearms—United States—Biography—Juvenile literature. 3. Frontier and pioneer
life—West (U.S.)—Juvenile literature. [1. Oakley, Annie, 1860-1926—Childhood and
youth. 2. Sharpshooters. 3. Women—Biography.] I. Title. II. Series: Ready-to-read
childhood of the famous Americans.
GV1157.03D58 2004
799.3'092—dc22   2003022392

Annie and John Mosey
ran through the barnyard.

"Hurry, John! Father is loading his wagon for the mill," shouted Annie. "He will be gone all day."

"We are just in time to say good-bye," said John.

"In town I will buy our food

 for the winter," said Father.

"Will you also bring us

 a gift, Father?" asked John.

"Wait and see, Son.

 I will be home for supper."

"We are going to build

a bird trap today," said Annie.

"Good! We will check on it

early tomorrow," said Father.

"Get along, horses!" he shouted.

As Father sped away, Annie and John met

Mother and the baby by the henhouse.

"It looks like snow," said Mother.

"I am worried about Father."

"He will make it safely home,"

said Annie. "He always does."

That afternoon, Annie and John

prepared their trap.

"Father uses corn stalks, string,

dried corn, and a stick,"

said Annie.

"Show me how," said John.

Annie broke the corn stalks
into even pieces and stacked
them on the ground.
The trap grew tall. It started
to look like a little log house.

"Father ties the corners to make
the trap strong," she said.
"He adds a roof so the bird
will not get out."
"How does the bird get in?"
asked John.

Annie held up the stick.

She dug a path uphill to the trap.

"Father drops corn along
  the path," she said.

"The stick will hold up the trap.

When the bird goes inside to eat,

it will knock down the stick

and be locked inside the trap."

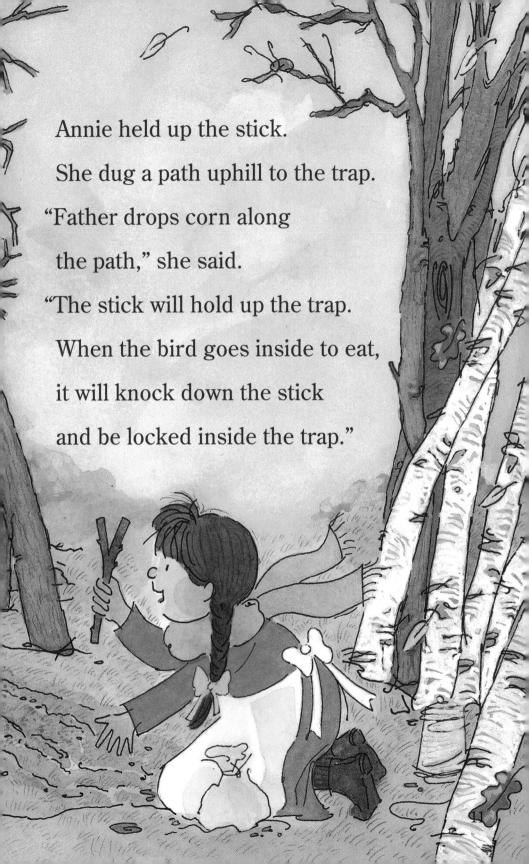

John sprinkled the corn.

"Hurry, Annie, it is

getting cold," he said.

"Let's go home."

"First we must hide our trap,"

she said.

They covered the trap with leaves
and started for the cabin.

"Father will be surprised when he
finds a fat bird in the trap
in the morning," said Annie.

"I want to find a fat bird
for supper tonight," said John.

The wind howled, *EEE OOO!*
John took Annie's hand.
Snowflakes began to swirl
around them.
"Will Father be home soon, Annie?"
asked John. "It is getting dark."
"Soon," she whispered. "Soon."

That night the family ate

soup for supper.

Boom! Wind shook the windows.

Crash! A tree branch fell.

John jumped in his chair.

"Mother, I am afraid!" he cried.

"It is a blizzard," she said.

"But we are safe at home, together."

The last log burned on the fire.

"Annie," said Mother, "I need you
to get more logs from the woodpile."

Mother tied one end of a rope

to the porch post, and the other

around Annie's waist.

Annie held on to the rope.

The wind pushed and
pulled her along.
At one point Annie slipped
and dropped the firewood.

Soon Annie could not see the
cabin through the snow.
Her fingers were numb, and her
face stung. But she hung on
until she was home with the wood.

Mother threw more wood on the fire,
and the children lay down to sleep.
"Let us pray for Father on this long,
snowy night," Annie said.
She lay awake listening
to the storm.
Suddenly Annie heard horses.
"Father is home!" she cried.

Mother threw the door wide open.

Father sat on his wagon

with the horses' reigns

wrapped around his wrists.

He did not speak

or move his hands.

"Father looks frozen!" cried Annie.

"The horses must have found

their own way home."

The family carried Father inside.

Annie took his wet coat.

A bag fell from the pocket.

"Father, you remembered," said John.

"Peppermints! Thank you."

Father shivered.

"Will he be all right?"

whispered Annie.

"I hope so," said Mother.

The next morning Annie and John
crept past Father while he slept.
"A bird from our trap will cheer
Father up today," said John.
"He will feel better!"

"Hush!" whispered Annie.

"Father must rest.

Let's hurry outside

before we wake him."

In the woods they brushed the snow
and leaves from the trap.

"I hear it!" said Annie. "Listen!"

"What is it, Annie?"

John leaned near the trap.

"Hoy, hoy!" sang a little voice.

"It's Molly, our hen!" said John.

"It's not Molly," laughed Annie.

"It's a quail!"

Annie held up the bird.

"Father will be proud!" said John.

Annie wrapped the quail in her scarf.

"Until Father feels better,

he can count on us to help

feed the family with our traps,"

she said.

"We can do it!" said John.

"We will!" said Annie.

And they did.

31

Annie, later known as Annie Oakley, trapped and hunted to help her family survive many hardships.

Here is a timeline of her life:

1860	Born Phoebe Anne Mosey, in Darke County, Ohio, on August 13
1866	Jacob Mosey, Annie's father, comes home nearly frozen. Dies from pneumonia February 11
1868	Annie shoots a gun for the first time
1875	Meets Frank Butler and beats him in a shooting match on Thanksgiving Day
1876	Marries Frank Butler on August 23
1882	First uses the stage name Annie Oakley in a trick-shooting match with her husband
1885	Joins Buffalo Bill's Wild West Show
1887	Performs with Buffalo Bill's Wild West Show in England, for Queen Victoria
1901	Injured in a train wreck in North Carolina; retires from Buffalo Bill's Wild West Show
1908	Susan Mosey Shaw, Annie's mother, dies
1911	Joins the Young Buffalo Show again
1913	Gives her last show as a Young Buffalo Show star and permanently retires from performing
1926	Dies on November 3, near the family farm in Greenville, Ohio; her husband dies only 18 days later in Michigan

READING ★ WITH ★ THE ★ STARS!

Simon Spotlight Ready-to-Read books showcase your favorite characters—the stars of these stories!

At every level, you are a reading star!

PRE-LEVEL ONE ★ RISING STAR READER!
Shared reading ★ Familiar characters ★ Simple words

LEVEL ONE ★ STAR READER!
Easy sight words and words to sound out ★ Simple plot and dialogue
Familiar topics and themes

LEVEL TWO ★ SUPERSTAR READER!
Longer sentences ★ Simple chapters ★ High-interest vocabulary words

LEVEL THREE ★ MEGASTAR READER!
Longer, more complex story plot and character development
Challenging vocabulary words ★ More difficult sentence structure

As young Annie Oakley—then Annie Mosey—sees her father off to the mill, she notices the gray sky. It looks like snow, which means a dangerous trip for Father. To take her mind off her worries, Annie shows her brother how to build a trap, just the way their father showed her. Little does she realize just how important this lesson will soon be. . . .

by Anna DiVito

Find more Ready-to-Read books at
ReadytoRead.com

ISBN 978-0-689-86520-6 **$4.99 U.S./**$6.99 Can.

50499

9 780689 865206

A Ready-to-Read Book/Nonfiction
SIMON SPOTLIGHT
Simon & Schuster, New York
1104

READY★TO★READ

LEVEL TWO

Childhood of Famous Americans

Helen Keller
and the Big Storm

written by Patricia Lakin · illustrated by Diana Magnuson

THEN REACH FOR THE STARS!

Each child is a rising star in our Ready-to-Read program, gaining confidence as they launch from one reading level to the next. With a constellation of engaging, soon-to-be favorite stories and starring characters to lead the way, we encourage beginning readers to enjoy the journey of learning to read.

The Ready-to-Read stories are grouped into four reading levels:

PRE-LEVEL ONE ★ RISING STAR READER!
Stories are shared reading experiences, featuring familiar characters and simple words.

LEVEL ONE ★ STAR READER!
Stories feature easy sight words and words to sound out, simple plot and dialogue, as well as familiar topics and themes.

LEVEL TWO ★ SUPERSTAR READER!
Stories have simple chapters, longer sentences, and high-interest vocabulary words.

LEVEL THREE ★ MEGASTAR READER!
Stories have longer, more complex plots and character development, challenging vocabulary words, and more difficult sentence structure.

Confidence is a big key to learning to read, and whether a child is a Rising Star or a Megastar, this program is designed to help kids feel like stars at **every** reading level. With the help of their favorite characters, every reading star will sparkle and shine as they take pride in their abilities and learn to love reading.

Blast off on this starry adventure . . . a universe of reading awaits!

Helen Keller
and the
Big Storm

written by
Patricia Lakin

illustrated by
Diana Magnuson

Ready-to-Read

Aladdin

New York   London   Toronto   Sydney   Singapore

For Erika Tamar . . .
who always brings me back to my senses.
—P.L.

To Samantha.
Thanks for making it real.
—D.M.

First Aladdin edition January 2002

Text copyright © 2002 by Patricia Lakin

Illustrations copyright © 2002 by Diana Magnuson

Aladdin Paperbacks

An imprint of Simon & Schuster

Children's Publishing Division

1230 Avenue of the Americas

New York, NY 10020

All rights reserved, including the right of

reproduction in whole or in part in any form.

CHILDHOOD OF FAMOUS AMERICANS is a registered trademark

of Simon & Schuster, Inc.

READY-TO-READ is a registered trademark of Simon & Schuster, Inc.

The text for this book was set in 17 Point Utopia

Designed by Lisa Vega

The illustrations were rendered in acrylic

Printed and bound in the United States of America

20 19

The Library of Congress has Cataloged the paperback edition as follows:
Lakin, Pat.
Helen Keller and the big storm / written by Patricia Lakin ; illustrated by Diana Magnuson.
p. cm.–(Childhood of famous Americans series)
Summary: A true incident in the life of young Helen Keller in which she gets stuck in a storm and her
teacher, Annie Sullivan, rescues her.
ISBN 978-0-689-84104-0 (pbk.)
0121 LAK
1. Keller, Helen, 1880-1968—Childhood and youth—Juvenile literature. 2. Blind-deaf women—United
States—Biography—Juvenile literature. 3. Sullivan, Annie, 1866-1936—Juvenile literature. [1. Keller,
Helen, 1880-1968—Childhood and youth. 2. Sullivan, Annie, 1866-1936. 3. Blind. 4. Deaf. 5. Physically
handicapped. 6. Women—Biography.] I. Magnuson, Diana, ill. II. Title. III. Series.
HV1624.K4 L34 2002
362.4'1'092—dc21
[B]
2001033818

Helen Keller
and the
Big Storm

Little Helen Keller loved
smelling roses and honeysuckle.
They grew all around
her Alabama home.

But most of all,
Helen loved playing pranks.
When she was six, she had done
her best prank yet!
Mamma had walked
into the
kitchen pantry.

Quickly, Helen felt for the key.
Click! Helen locked Mamma inside.
Helen didn't always have the chance
to take charge like that.
Mamma and Papa tried hard
to understand her.
But many times no one knew
what she wanted.

Helen could get so angry,
she would kick and hit
and fall into a heap.

Afterward, she ran outside.
She threw herself onto
the cool, comforting grass.
The flowers, trees, grass,
warm sun, and gentle wind
always made Helen feel better.

Helen was never punished
for her pranks and tantrums.
Mr. and Mrs. Keller thought
Helen had been punished enough.
Their daughter could not hear,
or see, or talk.
But that pantry prank
forever changed Helen's life.
The Kellers now knew
that Helen needed more
than they could give her.
She needed special lessons
from a special teacher.

Helen's teacher was Annie Sullivan.

She came to live with the Kellers.

Helen was not ready
to trust this stranger.
And she was not ready
to give up her pranks.
She locked Annie inside her room.
And this time Helen hid the key!
That prank made Annie see
just how clever Helen was.
No matter what Helen did,
Annie did not give up!

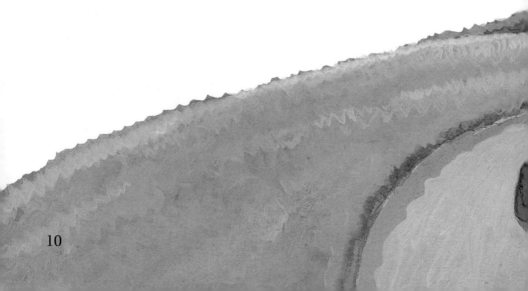

Slowly, day by day,
she worked with Helen.
Annie taught Helen
by pressing her fingers
into Helen's hand.
Annie's fingers spelled out the names
for the things Helen loved.
Grass. Flowers. Leaves. Trees. Bugs.
Butterflies. Sun. Wind. Rain.
In a short time, Helen loved
doing her lessons
more than doing her pranks.

Soon, the out-of-doors
became Helen's classroom.
One summer day,
Helen and Annie took a long walk.
On their way home,
the air grew hot and sticky.

Helen and Annie stopped to rest
under a wild cherry tree.
The tree blocked them
from the burning hot sun.
Its leaves fanned them
with a gentle, cooling breeze.

Helen felt its strong, low branches.

They were just right for climbing.

Annie and Helen decided to do just that!

Sitting high in the tree, they had
a resting-place to stay cool.
It was a perfect spot for a picnic!

Annie headed for the house

to make the lunch.

She made Helen promise

not to move an inch.

Helen wouldn't think of moving.

She loved sitting

high up in that tree!

Helen breathed in the wonderful scent
of the cherry tree.
She stroked its rough bark
and its smooth green leaves.
She let the cooling breeze blanket her.

But in seconds,
Helen's world
turned upside down.
The sun disappeared.
Helen's face was slapped
with a cold, sharp wind.

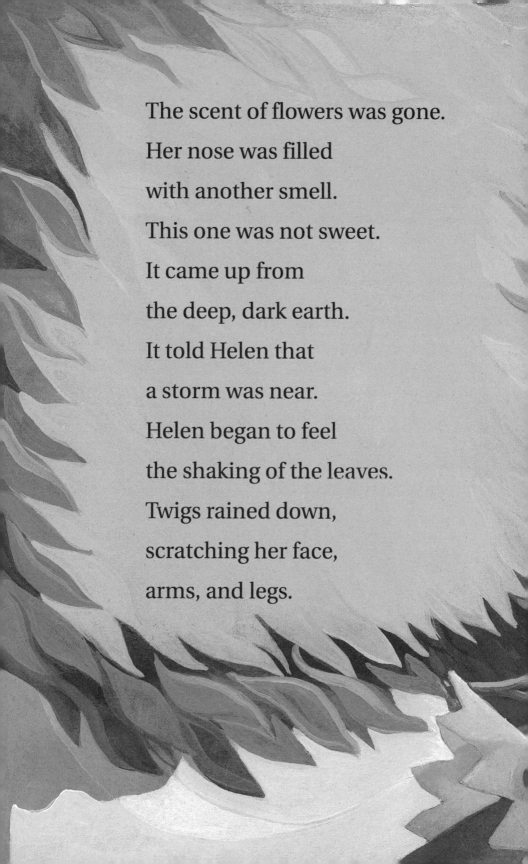

The scent of flowers was gone.

Her nose was filled

with another smell.

This one was not sweet.

It came up from

the deep, dark earth.

It told Helen that

a storm was near.

Helen began to feel

the shaking of the leaves.

Twigs rained down,

scratching her face,

arms, and legs.

Tree limbs swayed.
The wind whipped
through the branches.
The wind whipped
around Helen.
The wind tried to rip Helen
right out of that tree.

Helen grabbed onto
the shaking branch.
She clung to it
with all of her might.
Helen sat frozen.

She was trapped.

She could not see.

She could not call for help.

She could not hear

if help was on the way.

Helen had never felt

so alone or so scared.

She couldn't understand

how the gentle things she loved

could turn against her.

Suddenly, out of the
cold, whipping wind,
Helen felt a hand.
It was a strong, warm hand.
It belonged to Annie Sullivan.
Annie grabbed hold of Helen.
Helen let go of the branch.
She clung to Annie.
She let Annie guide her down
and out of that tree.

Helen learned
a great deal that day.
She had felt
the power of Nature.
It could turn
from gentle to fierce
in seconds.
Helen also learned
about the power of friendship.
Annie Sullivan would always
be there for Helen Keller.

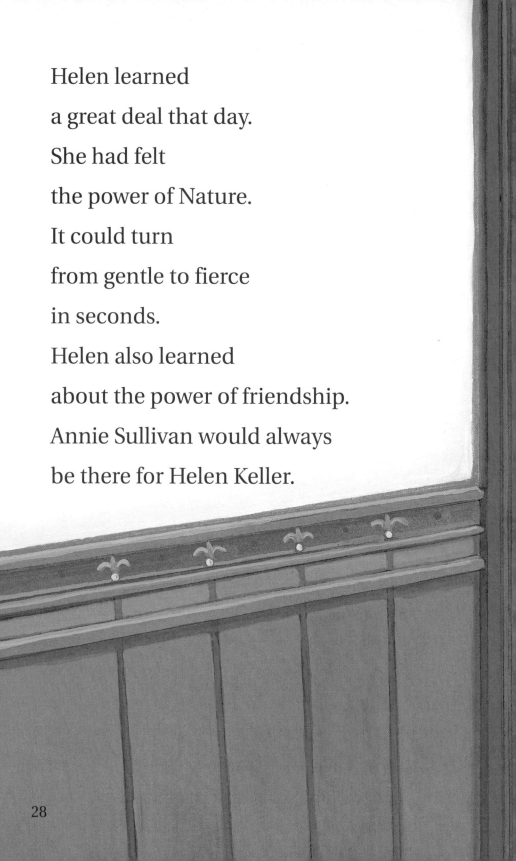

Helen Keller and Annie Sullivan
were friends all of their lives.
Helen went on to become
a talented writer
who always worked
to help others.

Here is a timeline of Helen's life:

1880   Helen is born in Alabama.

1882   Illness leaves her deaf and blind.

1887   Teacher Annie Sullivan arrives at the Kellers'.

1888   With Annie, attends Boston's Perkins Institute for the Blind for a more formal education.

1900   Enters Radcliffe College—now part of Harvard University.

1902   Autobiography of Helen's early years is published.

1904   Graduates with honors from Radcliffe.

1923   Begins lifelong role as world-traveling spokesperson for the disabled.

1931   Named one of the twelve greatest living American Women.

1936   Annie Sullivan dies, and Mary Agnes (Polly) Thompson becomes Helen's companion.

1959   Broadway play *The Miracle Worker* opens. It is based on Annie and Helen's early years together. In 1962 it is made into a major motion picture.

1964   Receives the United States's highest civilian award, The Presidential Medal of Freedom.

1968   Dies at home in Connecticut.